Scruffy & the Egg

Written and Illustrated by Angela M. Sanchez

Puppy & Sparrow Publishing

Puppy & Sparrow Publishing

5900 Wilshire Blvd., Suite 1540

Los Angeles, CA 90036

The illustrations were made with watercolor on paper.

Book design by Charles Allen Imaging Experts
Prepress and print management: Charles Allen Imaging Experts
Production files and retouching: Howard Morris (CAIE)
Printed in South Korea

Publisher's Cataloging-in-Publication Data

Names: Sanchez, Angela M.

Title: Scruffy and the egg / written and illustrated by Angela M. Sanchez.

Description: Los Angeles : Puppy & Sparrow, 2017. | Summary: An abandoned dog embarks on a
    quest to find his family and along the way meets an orphaned egg.

Identifiers: LCCN 2017942820 | ISBN 978-0-9979968-0-7 (hardcover) | ISBN 978-0-9979968-1-4 (pbk.) |
    ISBN 978-0-9979968-2-1 (ebook)

Subjects: LCSH: Single parents--Juvenile fiction. | Homeless families--Juvenile fiction. | CYAC: Dogs--
    Fiction. | Eagles--Fiction. | Self-realization--Fiction. | BISAC: JUVENILE FICTION / Animals /
    Dogs. | JUVENILE FICTION / Family / General. | JUVENILE FICTION / Social Themes /
    Homelessness & Poverty.

Classification: LCC PZ7.1.S259 Scr 2017 (print) | PZ7.1.S259 (ebook) | DDC [Fic]--dc23.

More Scruffy and the Egg adventures await at
www.angelamsanchez.com

10 9 8 7 6 5 4 3 2 1

For Dad, my Scruffy,
and with special thanks to all the people who
made sharing this story possible.

This is the Fluffy Dog.

His chestnut fur is always groomed until it shines. His bright, brown eyes sparkle.
It is clear that his family takes care of him.

He is a good dog, too. The Fluffy Dog always wipes his paws before coming inside.

He helps with chores and, of course, he's never too busy to play with the children. They are his favorite in the whole family.

The Fluffy Dog is also an obedient dog.

He fetches,

rolls over,

sits

. . . and stays.

Even when his family does not.

But he knows that loyal dogs stay and wait for their families. He is sure that his family will come back!

So he decides to stay and wait.

No matter what.

FORECLOSED

With no home and no one to take care of him,
he wanders the streets alone.

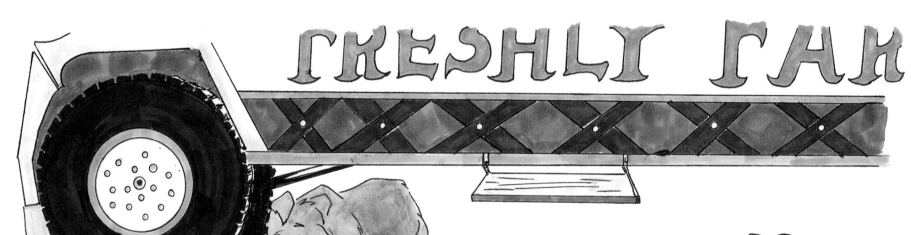

As his fur becomes matted and his paws become rough,
the Fluffy Dog becomes the Scruffy Dog.

His nose to the ground, Scruffy keeps sniffing, trying to pick up a scent that will lead him back to his family.

He wanders and wishes that maybe, just maybe, he will find his family again.

Scruffy keeps searching, but with each passing day he loses a little more hope. He looks everywhere—even high above the city.

He asks everyone.
But so far, not a single clue.

One day, Scruffy ventures a little farther out of town. After a long day, he falls asleep on a flat, warm rock.

He dreams of finding his family and seeing them again.

He probably would have slept straight through the day, until something large, white, and round falls out of the sky!

WHAM!! It crashes right into Scruffy's soft tummy.

Bouncing from his stomach and off his nose, the object lands safely on the ground with a *THUD!*

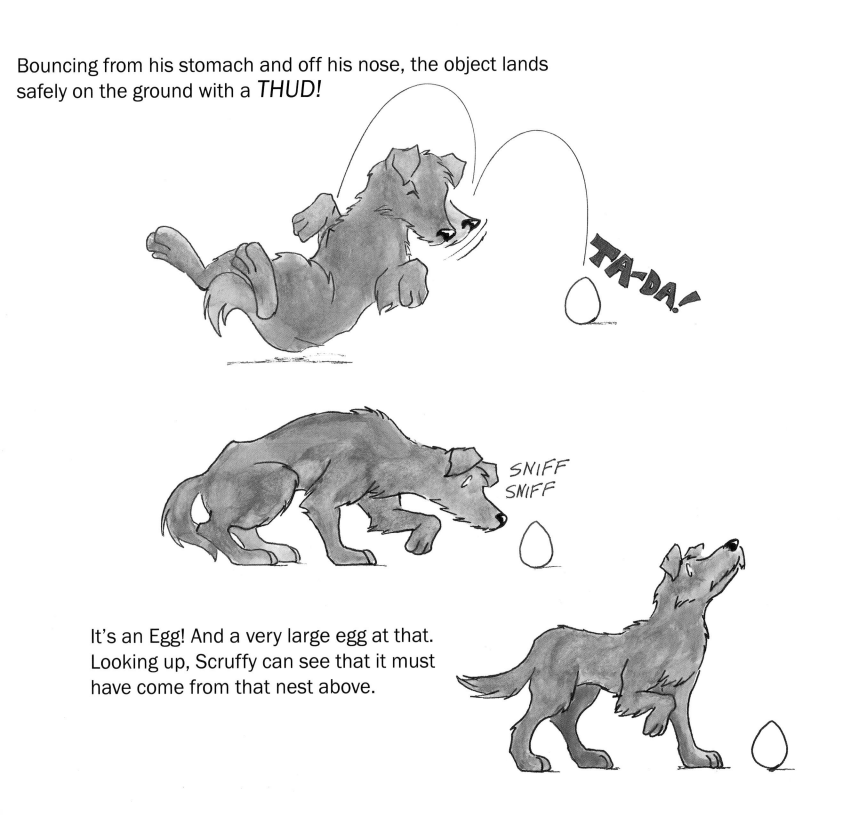

It's an Egg! And a very large egg at that. Looking up, Scruffy can see that it must have come from that nest above.

Way above!

"So, the Egg also has a family," Scruffy thinks. He decides to return it.

Gently, Scruffy pushes it up the cliff with his nose. But the Egg wobbles and sways. It won't go straight up.

The Egg is getting away! Faster and faster,
the Egg tumbles away from its home!

Scruffy springs into action. He doesn't want the Egg to crack!

With another bound and a leap, Scruffy catches up with the Egg.

Safely, he brings it to a gentle stop.

Scruffy needs to move on with his search.
He has a family to find.

But then he stops and thinks. He can't
leave the little Egg all alone. Scruffy
knows how that feels.

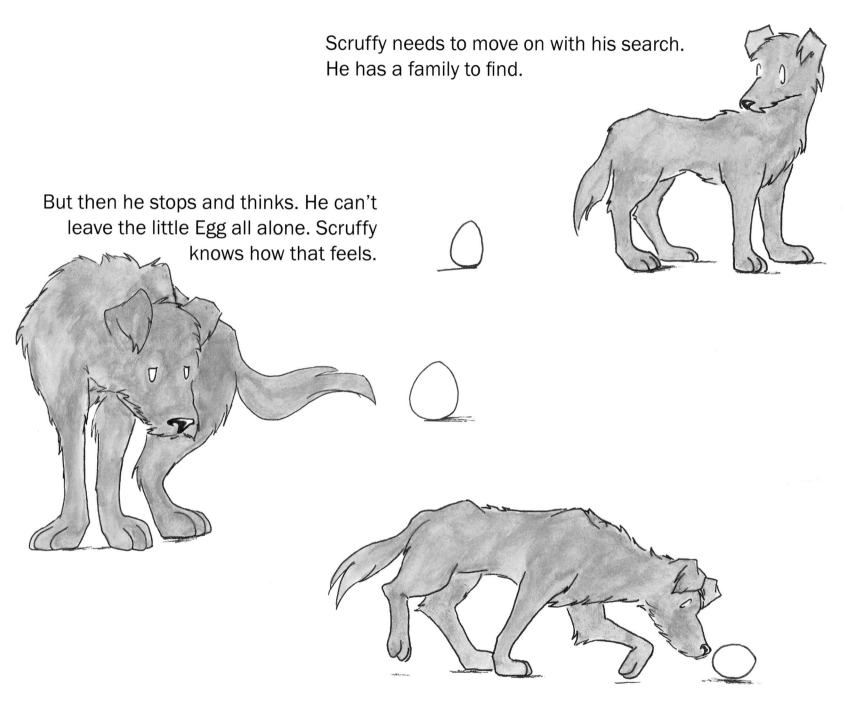

He makes another decision. He will take the Egg with him.

Scruffy pushes and rolls the Egg with his nose.
He hasn't forgotten about his family, but someone has to
take care of the Egg. Soon all he can think is, "Push the Egg."

And push he does.
Down the sidewalk,

across bridges,

past the basketball court

. . . and into the city.

But just as he pushes it to cross the street, the Egg rolls off course—and straight into traffic!

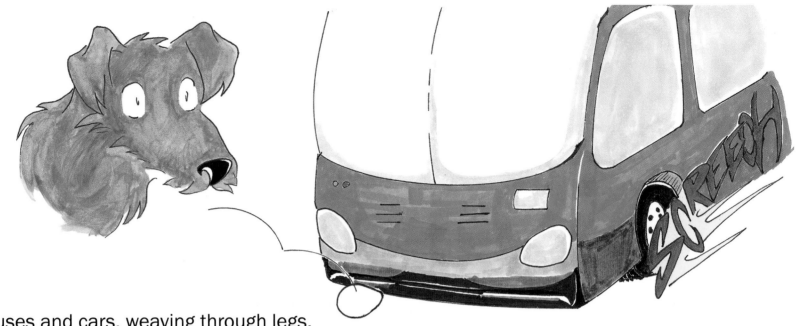

Dodging buses and cars, weaving through legs,

Scruffy chases after his Egg. He stops it
at the corner of the street. Just in time.

But before Scruffy can check for a
   single scratch, suddenly the Egg shakes!
   It quivers and cracks—the Egg is hatching!

First comes the beak with a loud, "Cheep!"

Then—with a loud *CRACK*—
   come the feet.

Scruffy is proud and happy to
see what comes next.

His tail wagging, Scruffy waits excitedly for the rest of the Egg to hatch.

But nothing else happens. That is all. It is still an Egg.

"Cheep!" says the Egg. On two skinny little legs, the Egg marches along, singing to itself.

"Cheep!
    Cheep, cheep, a-cheep!
        Cheep!"

Scruffy is surprised to see his Egg move on its own.
It looks as if it could take care of itself.

Scruffy feels sad that the Egg does not need him
anymore. He starts to leave.

"Cheep!" the Egg calls after Scruffy.

Scruffy hears the little feet scuttling behind him.

And he waits.

When he turns around, for the first time in what feels like a long time, Scruffy smiles.

Until the Egg races in front of him

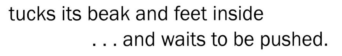

tucks its beak and feet inside
. . . and waits to be pushed.

"Cheep!" chirps the Egg.

It sounds like an order.

But Scruffy doesn't mind. When he was the Fluffy Dog, he could not have imagined meeting an Egg. Or how much that Egg would mean to him.

Scruffy was looking for his family, but it seems that his family found him.

Scruffy found his Egg.

Discussion Questions for Readers

- What do you think will happen next? Draw it if you can!

- When he can't put it back in the nest, Scruffy decides to take the Egg with him. Why do you think he does that?

- At the end of the story, Scruffy hasn't found his family yet, but he's still happy. Why do you think that is?

- What does family mean to you? Scruffy and the Egg don't look anything like each other. Can they still be a family?

  Remember: Scruffy doesn't look like his human family!

- Scruffy and the Egg don't have a home right now. Do families need a home in order to be a family? Why do you think so?

Talking About Homelessness with Young Readers

For most people, a home is a safe place where you can sleep, relax, and come and go as you want. When a person doesn't have a safe place to stay or if there are limits on how long they can stay there—such as at a shelter, a motel, or a friend's house—then that person is without a home. They are homeless.

People experience homelessness because they do not make enough money to pay for a place to live and to buy food, medicine, and clothing. There are people who have jobs and still do not have enough money for a home of their own.

Anybody can be homeless, including children. Out of every four people who are homeless, one is a child, usually about eight years old. Kids who are homeless usually have at least one parent with them, but sometimes they are on their own. They most likely have families, friends, and go to school. They might also have to change schools a lot because their families have to move from place to place. Sometimes it can be tough sharing these experiences and feelings with other kids who don't know what homelessness is or how they can help. Don't be afraid to find out and learn more!

For kids who are dealing with homelessness, you should know that the more you share about your story, the more help you can get and the stronger you will become. There are a lot of people and organizations who care about you and want to help. **YOU** are important!

To Learn More About and Find Resources for
Families and Kids Experiencing Homelessness:

School on Wheels, Inc. www.schoolonwheels.org

The National Alliance to End Homelessness https://endhomelessness.org/

National Center on Family Homelessness https://www.air.org/center/national-center-family-homelessness

The National Center for Homeless Education https://nche.ed.gov/

National Association for the Education of Homeless Children and Youth http://naecy.org/

No Place to Be: Voices of Homeless Children by Judith Berck